The
WISDOM
of
THE QUR'AN

The
WISDOM
of
THE QUR'AN

ONEWORLD

OXFORD

THE WISDOM OF THE QUR'AN

Oneworld Publications
(Sales and Editorial)
185 Banbury Road
Oxford OX2 7AR
England

http://www.oneworld-publications.com

Oneworld Publications
(US Marketing Office)
160 N. Washington St.
4th Floor, Boston
MA 02114
USA

© Oneworld Publications 2000

ISBN 1–85168–224–4

Cover design by Design Deluxe, Bath
Typeset by Cyclops Media Productions
Printed and bound by Graphicom Srl, Vicenza, Italy

CONTENTS

ACKNOWLEDGEMENTS

The publisher would like to thank the following institutions for assistance and permission to produce the following pictures:

Peter Sanders Photography (pp. 45, 49, 53, 93, 97, 104, 140, 144, 149, 157); The Art Archive (pp. 29, 57, 84, 108, 133, 153)

GOD

THE CREATOR

AND WITH Him are the keys of the Invisible.
None but He knoweth them.
And He knoweth what is in the land and
the sea.
Not a leaf falleth but He knoweth it,
not a grain amid the darkness of the earth,
naught of wet or dry but it is noted in a
clear record.

He it is Who gathereth you at night
and knoweth that which ye commit by day.
Then He raiseth you again to life therein,
that the term appointed for you may be
accomplished.
And afterward unto Him is your return.
Then He will proclaim unto you what ye
used to do.

VI: 59–60

READ: IN the name of thy Lord Who
   createth,
Createth man from a clot.
Read: And thy Lord is the Most Bounteous,
Who teacheth by the pen,
Teacheth man that which he knew not.
Nay, but verily man is rebellious
That he thinketh himself independent!
Lo! unto thy Lord is the return.

XCVI: 1–8

ALL THAT is in the heavens and the earth
   glorifieth God;
and He is the Mighty, the Wise.
His is the Sovereignty of the heavens and
   the earth;
He quickeneth and He giveth death;
and He is Able to do all things.
He is the First and the Last,
and the Outward and the Inward; and He is
   Knower of all things.

LVII: 1–3

IN THE name of God, the Beneficent, the
  Merciful.
Praise be to God, Lord of the Worlds,
The Beneficent, the Merciful.
Master of the Day of Judgement,
Thee alone we worship; Thee alone we ask
  for help.
Show us the straight path,
The path of those whom Thou hast
  favoured;
Not the path of those who earn Thine anger
  nor of those who go astray.

I: 1–7

SAY: O GOD! Owner of Sovereignty!
Thou givest sovereignty unto whom Thou
    wilt,
and Thou withdrawest sovereignty from
    whom Thou wilt.
Thou exaltest whom Thou wilt,
and Thou abasest whom Thou wilt.
In Thy hand is the good.
Lo! Thou art Able to do all things.

Thou causest the night to pass into the day,
and Thou causest the day to pass into the
    night.
And Thou bringest forth the living from the
    dead,
and Thou bringest forth the dead from the
    living.
And Thou givest sustenance to whom
    Thou choosest,
without reckoning.

III: 26–7

GOD! THERE is no God but Him, the Living,
the Eternal.
Neither slumber nor sleep overtaketh Him.
Unto Him belongeth whatsoever is in the
heavens and whatsoever is in the
earth. Who is he that intercedeth with
Him save by His leave?
He knoweth that which is in front of them
and that which is behind them, while
they comprehend nothing of His
knowledge save what He wills.
His throne includeth the heavens and the
earth, and He is never weary of
preserving them. He is the Sublime, the
All-Glorious.

II: 255

LO! IN the creation of the heavens and the
   earth
and in the difference of night and day
are tokens of His Sovereignty for men of
   understanding.
Such as remember God, standing, sitting,
   and reclining,
and consider the creation of the heavens
   and the earth,
and say: Our Lord! Thou hast not created
   this in vain.

III: 190–1

GLORIFIED IS HE, and Exalted above what
   they say!
The seven heavens and the earth and all
   that is therein praise Him,
and there is not a thing that does not
   proclaim His praise;
but ye understand not their praise.
Lo! He is ever Clement, All-Forgiving.

XVII: 43–4

VISION COMPREHENDETH Him not,
but He comprehendeth all vision.
He is the Subtle, the Aware.

VI: 103

VERILY WE created man from a product of
  wet earth;
Then placed him as a drop of seed in a safe
  lodging;
Then We created of the drop a clot,
then We created of the the clot a tissue,
then We created of the tissue bones,
then clothed the bones with flesh,
and then produced it as another creation.
So blessed be God, the Best of creators!
Then lo! after that ye surely die.
Then lo! on the Day of Resurrection ye
  are raised again.
And We have created above you seven
  paths, and We are never unmindful of
  creation.

XXIII: 12–17

HAVE NOT those who disbelieve known that
the heavens and the earth were of one
   piece,
then We parted them, and we made every
   living thing of water?
Will they not then believe?

And We have placed in the earth firm hills
lest it quake with them, and We
have placed therein ravines as roads
that haply they may find their way.

And We have made the sky a roof
   well-protected.
Yet they turn away from Our signs.
And He it is Who created the night and
   the day,
and the sun and the moon.
They float, each in an orbit.

XXI: 30–3

IS NOT He best Who created the heavens
and the earth,
and sendeth down for you water from the
sky
wherewith We cause to spring forth joyous
orchards,
whose trees it never hath been yours to
cause to grow.
Is there any god beside God? Nay,
but they are folk who ascribe equals unto
Him!

Is not He best Who made the earth a fixed
abode,
and placed rivers in the folds thereof,
and placed firm hills therein,
and hath set a barrier between the two
seas?
Is there any God beside God? Nay, but
most of them know not!

Is not He best Who answereth the wronged
one

when he crieth unto Him and removeth the
    evil,
and hath made you viceroys of the earth?
Is there any God beside God? Little do
    they reflect!

Is not He best Who guideth you in the
    darkness
of the land and the sea,
He Who sendeth the winds as heralds of His
    mercy?
Is there any god beside God?
High Exalted be God from all that they
    ascribe as partner unto Him!

Is not He best Who produceth creation,
    then reproduceth it,
and Who provideth for you from the
    heaven and the earth?
Is there any God beside God?
Say: Bring your proof, if ye are truthful!

XXVII: 60–4

GOD IS the Light of the heavens and the
earth.
The similitude of His light is as a niche
wherein is a lamp.
The lamp is in a glass.
The glass is as it were a shining
star. This lamp is kindled from a blessed
tree,
an olive neither of the East nor of the West,
whose oil would almost glow forth
though no fire touched it.
Light upon light.
God guideth unto His light whom He will.
And God speaketh to mankind in
allegories,
for God is Knower of all things.

XXIV: 35

 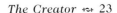

HAST THOU not seen that God,
He it is Whom all who are in the heavens
   and
the earth praise, and the birds in their
   flight?
Of each He knoweth verily the worship
   and the praise;
and God is Aware of what they do.
And unto God belongeth the Sovereignty
   of the heavens
and the earth, and unto God is the
   journeying.

XXIV: 41–2

SO GLORY be to God when ye enter the night
and when ye enter the morning.
Unto Him be praise in the heavens and the
   earth!
and at the sun's decline and in the
   noonday.

He bringeth forth the living from the dead,
and He bringeth forth the dead from the
living,
and He reviveth the earth after her death.
And even so will ye be brought forth.

XXX: 17–19

GOD IT is Who created the heavens and the
earth,
and that which is between them, in six
Days.
Then seated Himself upon the Throne.
Ye have not, beside Him, a protecting
friend or mediator.
Will ye not then remember?
He directeth the affair from the heaven
unto the earth;
then it ascendeth unto Him in a Day,
whereof the measure is a thousand
years of your counting.

XXXII: 4–5

HAVE YE seen that which ye cultivate?
Is it ye who foster it, or are We the
Fosterer?
If We willed, We verily could make it chaff,
then would ye cease not to exclaim:
Lo! we are laden with debt!
Nay, but we are deprived!

Have ye observed the water which ye
drink?
Is it ye who shed it from the raincloud,
or are We the Shedder?
If We willed We verily could make it bitter.
Why then, give ye not thanks?

Have ye observed the fire which ye kindle;
Was it ye who made the tree thereof to
grow,
or were We the grower?
We, even We, appointed it a reminder and
a comfort
for the dwellers in the wilderness.

LVI: 63–73

The Creator 27

AND OF His signs is this: He created you of
    dust,
and behold you human beings, ranging
    widely!

And of His signs is this: He created for you
helpmeets from yourselves that ye might
    find rest in them,
and He ordained between you love and
    mercy.
Lo! herein indeed are portents for folk who
    reflect.

And of His signs is the creation of the
    heavens
and the earth, and the difference of your
    languages and colours.
Lo! herein indeed are portents for men of
    knowledge.

And of His signs is your slumber by night
    and by day,
and your seeking of His bounty.

Lo! herein indeed are portents for folk who
heed.

And of His signs is this: He showeth you the
lightning
for a fear and for a hope, and sendeth
down water from the sky,
and thereby quickeneth the earth after her
death.
Lo! herein indeed are portents for folk who
understand.

XXX: 20–4

HE IS God, there is no other god but He, the
Knower of the Invisible and the Visible.
He is the Beneficent, Merciful.

He is God, there is no other god but He,
the Sovereign Lord, the Holy One, Peace,
the Keeper of Faith,
the Guardian, the Majestic, the Compeller,
the Superb.
Glorified be God from all that they ascribe
as partner unto Him.

He is God, the Creator, the Shaper out of
   naught,
the Fashioner. His are the most beautiful
   names.
All that is in the heavens and the earth
glorifieth Him, and He is the Mighty, the Wise.

LIX: 22–4

HAST THOU not seen that God knoweth all
that is in the heavens and all that is in the
   earth?
There is no secret conference of three but
He is their fourth, nor of five but He is their
   sixth,
nor of less than that or more but He is with
   them
wheresoever they may be; and afterward,
   on the Day of Resurrection,
He will inform them of what they did.
Lo! God is Knower of all things.

LVIII: 7

SUBMISSION TO GOD

O YE WHO believe! Come, all of you, into submission unto Him; and follow not the footsteps of the devil. Lo! he is an open enemy for you.

And if ye slide back after the clear proofs have come unto you, then know that God is Mighty, Wise.

II: 208–9

W HO IS better in religion than he who surrendereth his purpose to God while doing good to men and followeth the tradition of Abraham, the upright? God Himself chose Abraham for a friend.

IV: 125

SAY: LO! As for me, my Lord hath guided me unto a straight path, a right religion, the community of Abraham, the upright, who was no idolater.

Say: Lo! my worship and my sacrifice and my living and my dying are for God, Lord of the Worlds.

He hath no partner. This am I commanded, and I am first of those who surrender unto Him.

VI: 161–3

HE WHO obeyeth God and His messenger, and feareth God, and keepeth duty unto Him: such indeed are the victorious.

They swear by God solemnly that, if thou order them, they will go forth. Say: Swear not; honourable obedience is better. Lo! God is Informed of what ye do.

XXIV: 52–3

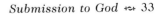

L O! THOU canst not make the dead to hear, nor canst thou make the deaf to hear the call when they have turned to flee;

Nor canst thou lead the blind out of their error. Thou canst make none to hear, save those who believe Our revelations and who have surrendered.

XXVII: 80–1

THEY MAKE it a favour unto thee Muhammad that they have surrendered unto Him. Say: Deem not your Surrender a favour unto me; but God doth confer a favour on you, inasmuch as He hath led you to the Faith, if ye are earnest.

XLIX: 17

TRUST IN GOD'S MERCY

THE DEVIL promiseth you destitution and enjoineth on you lewdness. But God promiseth you forgiveness from Himself with bounty. God is All-Embracing, All-Knowing.

II: 268

IF GOD is your helper none can overcome you, and if He withdraw His help from you, who is there who can help you after Him? In God let believers put their trust.

III: 160

AND IF a provocation from Satan should provoke thee, then seek refuge in God. Lo! He is All-Hearing, All-Seeing. The God-fearing, when a visitation of Satan troubles them, remember, and then see clearly.

VII: 200–1

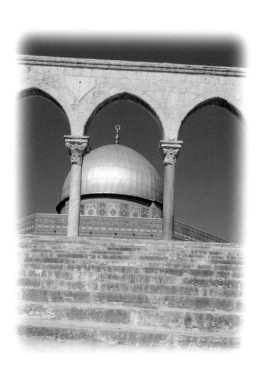

AND RECITE that which hath been revealed unto thee of the Scripture of thy Lord. There is none who can change His words, and thou wilt find no refuge beside Him.

XVIII: 27

PUT THY trust in the Living God,
the Undying,
and proclaim His praise.

XXV: 58

AND HE it is Who accepteth repentance from His servants, and pardoneth the evil deeds, and knoweth what ye do, And accepteth those who do good works, and giveth increase unto them of His bounty.

XLII: 25–6

WHO IS he that will lend unto God a goodly loan, that He may double it for him and his may be a rich reward?

LVII: 11

SAY: O My servants who have been prodigal to their own hurt! Despair not of the mercy of God, Who forgiveth all sins. Lo! He is the Forgiving, the Merciful.

Turn unto your Lord repentant, and surrender unto Him, before there come unto you the doom, when ye cannot be helped.

And follow the better guidance of that which is revealed unto you from your Lord, before the doom cometh on you suddenly when ye know not,

Lest any soul should say: Alas, my grief that I was unmindful of God, and I was indeed among the scoffers!

Or should say: If God had but guided me I should have been among the dutiful!

Or should say, when it seeth the doom: Oh, that I had but a second chance that I might be among the righteous!

But now the answer will be: Nay, for My revelations came unto thee, but thou didst deny them and wast scornful and wast among the disbelievers.

XXXIX: 53–9

RACE ONE with another for forgiveness from your Lord and a Garden whereof the breadth is as the breadth of the heavens and the earth, which is in store for those who believe in God and His messengers. Such is the bounty of God, which He bestoweth upon whom He will, and God is of Infinite Bounty.

LVII: 21

O YE WHO believe! Be mindful of your duty to God and put faith in His messenger. He will give you twofold of His mercy and will appoint for you a light wherein ye shall walk, and will forgive you. God is Forgiving, Merciful.

LVII: 28

AND WHOSOEVER keepeth his duty to God, God will appoint a way out for him, and will provide for him in a way that he cannot foresee.

And whosoever putteth his trust in God, He will suffice him. Lo! God bringeth His command to pass. God hath set a measure for all things.

LXV: 2–3

AND VERILY thy Lord will give unto thee so
  that thou wilt be content.
Did He not find thee an orphan and protect
  thee?
Did He not find thee wandering and direct
  thee?
Did He not find thee destitute and enrich
  thee?
Therefore the orphan oppress not,
Therefore the beggar drive not away,
Therefore of the bounty of thy Lord be thy
  discourse.

XCIII: 5–11

REVELATION

MESSENGERS OF GOD

S AY O MUSLIMS: We believe in God and that which is revealed unto us and that which was revealed unto Abraham, and Ishmael, and Isaac, and tribes, and that which Moses and Jesus received, and that which the prophets received from their Lord. We make no distinction between any of them, and unto Him we have surrendered.

II: 136

W E HAVE sent unto you a messenger from among you, who reciteth unto you Our revelations and causeth you to grow, and teacheth you the Scripture and wisdom, and teacheth you that which ye knew not.

Therefore remember Me, I will remember you. Give thanks to Me, and reject not Me.

II: 151–2

AND WE caused Jesus, son of Mary, to follow in their footsteps, confirming that which was revealed before him in the Torah, and We bestowed on him the Gospel wherein is guidance and a light, confirming that which was revealed before it in the Torah – a guidance and an admonition unto those who ward off evil.

Let the People of the Gospel judge by that which God hath revealed therein. Whoso judgeth not by that which God hath revealed: such are the ungodly.

And unto thee have We revealed the Scripture with the truth, confirming whatever Scripture was before it, and a watcher over it. So judge between them by that which God hath revealed, and follow not their desires away from the truth which hath come unto thee. For each We have appointed a divine law and a traced-out way. Had God willed He could have made you one community. But that He may try you by that which He hath given you He hath made you as ye are. So vie one with another in good works. Unto God ye will all return, and He will then inform you of that wherein ye differ.

V: 46–8

THE JEWS SAY: God's hand is fettered. Their hands are fettered and they are accursed for saying so. Nay, but both His hands are spread out wide in bounty. He bestoweth as He will.

V: 64

THERE IS no compulsion in religion. The right direction is henceforth distinct from error.

II: 256

THIS DAY have I perfected your religion for you and completed My favour unto you, and have chosen for you as religion al-Islam.

V: 3

O MESSENGER! Make known that which hath been revealed unto thee from thy Lord, for if thou do it not, thou wilt not have conveyed His message. God will protect thee from mankind.

V: 67

ND EVERY nation hath its term, and when its term cometh, they cannot put it off an hour nor yet advance it.

O Children of Adam! When messengers from among you come unto you who narrate unto you My revelations, then whosoever refraineth from evil and amendeth – there shall no fear come upon them neither shall they grieve.

But they who deny Our revelations and scorn them – each are rightful owners of the Fire; they will abide therein.

Who doeth greater wrong than he who inventeth a lie concerning God or denieth Our tokens?

VII: 34–7

SO SET thy face O Muhammad to the religion, as a man of pure faith, this is the primordial religion on which God has originated mankind. There is no altering God's creation. That is the right religion, but most men know it not.

Turning unto Him only; and be careful of your duty unto Him and perform the prayer, and be not of the idolaters,

Even of those who split up their religion and become sects, each sect exulting in its tenets.

XXX: 30–2

SAY O MUHAMMAD: O mankind! If ye are in doubt of my religion, then know that I worship not those whom ye worship instead of God, but I worship God Who causeth you to die, and I have been commanded to be of the believers.

And, O Muhammad set thy purpose resolutely for religion, as a man by nature upright, and be not of those who ascribe partners to God. And cry not, beside God, unto that which cannot profit thee nor hurt thee, for if thou didst so then wert thou of the wrong-doers. If God afflicteth thee with some hurt, there is none who can remove it save Him; and if He desireth good for thee, there is none who can repel His bounty. He striketh with it whom He will of his servants. He is the Forgiving, the Merciful.

Say: O mankind! Now hath the Truth from your Lord come unto you. So whosoever is guided, is guided only for the good of his soul, and whosoever erreth erreth only against it. And I am not a warder over you.

And O Muhammad follow that which is inspired in thee, and forbear until God give judgement. And He is the Best of Judges.

X: 104–9

A ND VERILY we have raised in every nation a messenger, proclaiming: Serve God and shun false gods.

XVI: 36

W ITH TRUTH have We sent it down, and with truth hath it descended. And We have sent thee as naught else save a bearer of good tidings and a warner.

And it is a Qur'an that We have divided, that thou mayst recite it unto mankind at intervals, and We have revealed it by successive revelation.

Say: Believe therein or believe not, lo! those who were given knowledge before it, when it is read unto them, fall down prostrate on their faces, adoring,

Saying: Glory to our Lord! Verily the promise of our Lord must be fulfilled.

They fall down on their faces, weeping, and it increaseth humility in them.

Say: Call upon God, or call upon the Merciful; whichsoever ye call upon, to Him belong the Names Most Beautiful.

XVII: 105–10

AND THOSE who disbelieve are driven unto hell in troops till, when they reach it and the gates thereof are opened, and the warders thereof say unto them: Came there not unto you messengers of your own, reciting unto you the revelations of your Lord and warning you of the meeting of this your Day? they say: Yea, verily. But the word of doom of disbelievers is fulfilled.

It is said unto them: Enter ye the gates of hell to dwell therein. Thus hapless is the journey's end of the scorners. And those who keep their duty to their Lord are driven unto the Garden in troops till, when they reach it, and the gates thereof are opened, and the warders thereof say unto them: Peace be unto you! Ye are good, so enter ye the Garden of delight, to dwell therein; they say: Praise be to God, Who hath fulfilled His promise unto us and hath made us inherit the land, sojourning in the Garden where we will! So bounteous is the wage of workers.

XXXIX: 71–4

LO! WE have shown man the way, whether he be grateful or disbelieving.

LXXVI: 3

VERILY WE sent messengers before thee, among them those of whom We have told thee, and some of whom We have not told thee; and it was not given to any messenger that he should bring a portent save by God's leave, but when God's commandment cometh the cause is judged aright, and the followers of vanity will then be lost.

XL: 78

WE VERILY sent Our messengers with clear proofs, and revealed with them the Scripture and the Balance, that mankind might uphold justice.

LVII: 25

THAT THE People of the Scripture may know that they control naught of the bounty of God, but that the bounty is in God's hand to give to whom He will. And God is of Infinite Bounty.

LVII: 29

THE CALL TO REMEMBRANCE

B<small>UT WHEN</small> there come unto you from Me a guidance, then whoso followeth My guidance, he will not go astray nor come to grief.

But he who turneth away from remembrance of Me, his will be a narrow life, and I shall bring him blind to the assembly on the Day of Resurrection.

He will say: My Lord! Wherefore hast Thou raised me blind, when I was wont to see?

He will say: So it must be. Our revelations came unto thee but thou didst forget them. In like manner thou art forgotten this Day.

XX: 123–6

IS IT not a guidance for them to know how many a generation We destroyed before them, amid whose dwellings they walk? Lo! therein verily are signs for men of thought.

XX: 128

SAY O MUHAMMAD, unto mankind: I warn you only by the Inspiration. But the deaf hear not the call when they are warned.

XXI: 45

WE SENT thee not O Muhammad save as a mercy for the peoples.
Say: It is revealed unto me only that your God is One God. Will ye then surrender unto Him?
But if they are averse, then say: I have warned you all alike, although I know not whether nigh or far is that which ye are promised.

XXI: 107–9

A S FOR those who disbelieve, their deeds are as a mirage in a desert. The thirsty one supposeth it to be water till he cometh unto it and findeth it naught, and findeth, in the place thereof, God Who payeth him his due; and God is swift at reckoning.

Or as darkness on a vast, abysmal sea. There covereth him a wave, above which is a wave, above which is a cloud. Layer upon layer of darkness. When he holdeth out his hand he scarce can see it. And he for whom God hath not appointed light, for him there is no light.

XXIV: 39–40

O YE WHO believe! Shall I show you a commerce that will save you from a painful doom?

Ye should believe in God and His messenger, and should strive for the cause of God with your wealth and your lives. That is better for you, if ye did but know.

He will forgive you your sins and bring you into Gardens underneath which rivers flow, and pleasant dwellings in Gardens of Eden. That is the supreme triumph.

LXI: 10–12

THE HOUR drew nigh and the moon was rent
    in twain.
And if they behold a portent they turn
    away and say: Prolonged illusion.
They denied the Truth and followed their
    own lusts. Yet everything will come to a
    decision
And surely there hath come unto them
    news whereof the purport should deter,
Effective wisdom; but warnings avail not.

LIV: 1–5

WILL THEY not regard the camels, how they
    are created?
And the heaven, how it is raised?
And the hills, how they are set up?
And the earth, how it is spread?
Remind them, for thou art but a reminder,
Thou art not charged to oversee them.

LXXXVIII: 17–22

MUHAMMAD

UHAMMAD IS but a messenger, messengers the like of whom have passed away before him. Will it be that, when he dieth or is slain, ye will turn back on your heels? He who turneth back on his heels doth no hurt to God, and God will reward the thankful.

III: 144

E HAVE sent thee Muhammad as a messenger unto mankind and God is sufficient as Witness.
Whoso obeyeth the messenger hath obeyed God, and whoso turneth away: We have not sent thee as a warder over them.

IV: 79–80

THE GUIDING of them is not thy duty O Muhammad, but God guideth whom He will.

II: 272

WE KNOW well how their talk grieveth thee, though in truth they deny not thee Muhammad but evil-doers deny the revelations of God.

Messengers indeed have been denied before thee, and they were patient under the denial and the persecution till Our succour reached them. There is none to alter the words of God. Already there hath reached thee some of the tidings of the messengers We sent before.

And if their aversion is grievous unto thee, then, if thou canst, seek a way down into the earth or a ladder unto the sky that thou mayest bring unto them a sign to convince them all! – If God willed, He could have brought them all together to the guidance – So be not thou among the foolish ones.

VI: 33–5

L O! HE Who hath given thee the Qur'an for a law will surely bring thee home again. Say: My Lord is best aware of him who bringeth guidance and him who is in manifest error.

Thou hadst no hope that the Scripture would be inspired in thee; but it is a mercy from thy Lord.

XXVIII: 85–6

A ND WHEN thou saidst unto him on whom God hath conferred favour and thou hast conferred favour: Keep thy wife to thyself, and fear God. And thou didst hide in thy mind that which God was to bring to light, and thou didst fear mankind whereas God hath a better right that thou shouldst fear Him. So when Zeyd had performed that necessary formality (of divorce) from her, We gave her unto thee in marriage, so that (henceforth) there may be no sin for believers in respect of wives of their adopted sons, when the latter have performed the necessary formality (of release) from them ... Muhammad is not the father of any man among you, but he is the messenger of God and the Seal of the Prophets; and God is ever Aware of all things.

XXXIII: 37–40

IT IS A Scripture that is revealed unto thee Muhammad – so let there be no heaviness in thy heart therefrom – that thou mayst warn thereby, and it is a Reminder unto believers.

VII: 2

SAY O MUHAMMAD, to the disbelievers: I say not unto you that I possess the treasures of God, nor that I have knowledge of the Unseen; and I say not unto you: Lo! I am an angel. I follow only that which is inspired in me.

VI: 50

O PROPHET! LO! We have sent thee as a witness and a bringer of good tidings and a warner.

And as a summoner unto God by His permission, and as a lamp that giveth light.

And announce unto the believers the good tidings that they will have great bounty from God.

And incline not to the disbelievers and the hypocrites. Disregard their noxious talk, and put thy trust in God. God is sufficient as Trustee.

XXXIII: 45–8

Muhammad ﷺ 61

AND IT was not vouchsafed to any mortal that God should speak to him unless it be by revelation or from behind a veil, or that He sendeth a messenger to reveal what He will by His leave. Lo! He is Exalted, Wise.

And thus have We inspired in thee Muhammad a Spirit of Our command. Thou knewest not what the Scripture was, nor what the Faith. But We have made it a light whereby We guide whom We will of Our servants. And lo! thou verily dost guide unto a right path.

XLII: 51–2

BY THE Star when it setteth,
Your comrade Muhammad erreth not, nor
    is deceived;
Nor doth he speak of his own desire.
It is naught save a revelation revealed,
Taught him by a mighty power,
One vigorous; and he stood poised,
When he was on the uppermost horizon.
Then he drew nigh and came down
Till he was two bows' length away or even
    nearer,

And He revealed unto His servant that
which He revealed.
His heart lied not in seeing what it saw.
Will ye then dispute with him concerning
what he saw?
And verily he saw him yet another time
By the Lote-Tree of the Utmost Boundary,
Nigh unto which is the Garden of Refuge.
When that which covereth did cover the
Lote-Tree,
His eye turned not aside nor swept astray.
Verily he saw one of the greatest
revelations of his Lord.

LIII: 1–18

THOU ART not O Muhammad, for thy Lord's
favour unto thee, a madman.
And lo! thine verily will be a reward
unfailing.
And lo! thou art of a great moral character.

LXVIII: 2–4

THE WORD

GOD OBLITERATES whatever verses He chooses, and confirms others, for with Him is the Mother of all Books.

XIII: 39

SAY: THOUGH the sea became ink for the Words of my Lord, verily the sea would be used up before the words of my Lord were exhausted, even though We brought the like thereof to help.

XVIII: 109

AND WHEN We put a revelation in place of another revelation – and God knoweth best what He revealeth – they say: Lo! thou art but inventing. Most of them know not.

XVI: 101

THUS WE have revealed it as a Lecture in Arabic, and have displayed therein certain threats, that peradventure they may keep from evil or that it may cause them to take heed.

Then exalted be God, the True King! And hasten not O Muhammad with the Qur'an ere its revelation hath been perfected unto thee, and say: My Lord! Increase me in knowledge.

XX: 113–14

IF WE had caused this Qur'an to descend upon a mountain, thou O Muhammad verily wouldst have seen it humbled, rent asunder by the fear of God. Such similitudes coin We for mankind that haply they may reflect.

LIX: 21

OTHER FAITHS

AND THEY say: None entereth paradise
    unless he be a Jew or a Christian.
These are their own desires.
Say: Bring your proof of what ye state if ye
    are truthful.
Nay, but whosoever surrendereth his
    purpose to God
while doing good, his reward is with his
    Lord;
and there shall no fear come upon them
    neither shall they grieve.
And the Jews say the Christians follow not
    the truth,
and the Christians say the Jews follow not
    truth;
yet both are readers of the Scripture.

II: 111–13

LO! THOSE who believe in that which is
    revealed unto thee, Muhammad, and
    those who are Jews, and Christians,
And Sabaeans – whoever believeth in God
And the Last Day and doeth right –
Surely their reward is with their Lord, and
    there
Shall no fear come upon them neither
    shall they grieve.

II: 62

AND THE Jews will not be pleased with thee, nor will the
Christians, till thou follow their creed. Say: Lo! the
guidance of God Himself is Guidance.

II: 120

SAY: O PEOPLE of the Scripture! Come to an agreement between us and you: that we shall worship none but God, and that we shall ascribe no partner unto Him, and that none of us shall take others for lords beside God.

III: 64

O PEOPLE OF the Scripture! Do not exaggerate in your religion nor utter aught concerning God save the truth. The Messiah, Jesus son of Mary, was only a messenger of God, and His word which He conveyed unto Mary, and a spirit from Him. So believe in God and His messengers, and say not 'Three' – Cease! It is better for you! – God is only One God. Far is it removed from His Transcendent Majesty that He should have a son. His is all that is in the heavens and all that is in the earth. And God is sufficient as Defender.

The Messiah will not be too proud to be God's servant, nor will the favoured angels. Whoso scorneth His service and is proud, all such will He assemble unto Him.

IV: 171–2

THEY SURELY disbelieve who say: Lo! God is the Messiah, son of Mary. The Messiah himself said: O Children of Israel, worship God, my Lord and your Lord. Lo! whoso ascribeth partners unto God, for him God hath forbidden paradise. His abode is the Fire. For evil-doers there will be no helpers.

They surely disbelieve who say: Lo! God is the third of three; when there is no God save the One God. If they desist not from so saying a painful doom will fall on those of them who disbelieve.

Will they not rather turn unto God and seek forgiveness of Him? For God is Forgiving, Merciful.

The Messiah, son of Mary, was no other than a messenger, messengers the like of whom had passed away before him. And his mother was a saintly woman. And they both used to eat earthly food. See how We make the revelations clear for them, and see how they are turned away!

V: 72–5

WHEN GOD saith: O Jesus, son of Mary! Remember My favour unto thee and unto thy mother; how I strengthened thee with the holy Spirit, so that thou spakest unto mankind in the cradle as in maturity; and how I taught thee the Scripture and Wisdom and the Torah and the Gospel; and how thou didst shape of clay as it were the likeness of a bird by My permission, and didst blow upon it and it was a bird by My permission, and thou didst heal him who was born blind and the leper by My permission; and how thou didst raise the dead by My permission; and how I restrained the Children of Israel from harming thee when thou camest unto them with clear proofs, and those of them who disbelieved exclaimed: This is naught else than mere magic.

And when I inspired the disciples, saying: Believe in Me and in My messenger, they said: We believe. Bear witness that we have surrendered unto Thee 'we are Muslims'.

When the disciples said: O Jesus, son of Mary! Is thy Lord able to send down for us a table spread with food from heaven? He said: Observe your duty to God, if ye are true believers.

They said: We wish to eat thereof, that we may satisfy our hearts and know that thou hast spoken truth to us, and that thereof we may be witnesses.

Jesus, son of Mary, said: O God, Lord of us! Send down for us a table spread with food from heaven, that it may be a feast for us, for the first of us and for the last of us, and a sign from Thee. Give us sustenance, for Thou art the Best of Sustainers.

God said: Lo! I send it down for you. And whoso afterward disbelieveth you, him surely will I punish with a punishment wherewith I have not punished any of My creatures.

And when God saith: O Jesus, son of Mary! Didst thou say unto mankind: Take me and my mother for two gods beside God? he saith: Be glorified! It was not mine to utter that to which I had no right. If I used to say it, then Thou knewest it.

Thou knowest what is in my mind, and I know not what is in Thy Mind. Lo! Thou, only Thou, art the Knower of Things Hidden.

I spake unto them only that which Thou commandedst me, saying: Worship God, my Lord and your Lord. I was a witness of them while I dwelt among them, and when Thou tookest me Thou wast the Watcher over them. Thou art Witness over all things.

If Thou punish them, lo! they are Thy servants, and if Thou forgive them lo! they are Thy servants. Lo! Thou, only Thou, art the Mighty, the Wise.

God saith: This is a day in which their truthfulness profiteth the truthful, for theirs are Gardens underneath which rivers flow, wherein they are secure for ever, God taking pleasure in them and they in Him. That is the great triumph.

Unto God belongeth the Sovereignty of the heavens and the earth and whatsoever is therein, and He is Able to do all things.

V: 110–20

AND MAKE mention of Mary in the Scripture, when she had withdrawn from her people to a chamber looking East, and had chosen seclusion from them. Then We sent unto her Our Spirit and it assumed for her the likeness of a perfect man.

She said: Lo! I seek refuge in the Beneficent One from thee, if thou art God-fearing.

He said: I am only a messenger of thy Lord, that I may bestow on thee a faultless son.

She said: How can I have a son when no mortal hath touched me, neither have I been unchaste?

He said: So it will be. Thy Lord saith: It is easy for Me. And it will be that We may make of him a revelation for mankind and a mercy from Us, and it is a thing ordained.

And she conceived him, and she withdrew with him to a far place.

And the pangs of childbirth drove her unto the trunk of the palm-tree. She said: Oh, would that I had died ere this and had become a thing of naught, forgotten!

Then one cried unto her from below her, saying: Grieve not! Thy Lord hath placed a rivulet beneath thee, And shake the trunk of the palm-tree toward thee, thou wilt cause ripe dates to fall upon thee.

So eat and drink and be consoled. And if thou meetest any mortal, say: Lo! I have vowed a fast unto the Beneficent, and may not speak this day to any mortal.

Then she brought him to her own folk, carrying him. They said: O Mary! Thou hast come with an amazing thing.

O sister of Aaron! Thy father was not a wicked man nor was thy mother a harlot.

Then she pointed to him. They said: How can we talk to one who is in the cradle, a young boy?

He spake: Lo! I am the servant of God. He hath given me the Scripture and hath appointed me a Prophet,

And hath made me blessed wheresoever I may be, and hath enjoined upon me prayer and almsgiving so long as I remain alive,

And hath made me dutiful toward her who bore me, and hath not made me arrogant, unblest.

Peace on me the day I was born, and the day I die, and the day I shall be raised alive!

Such was Jesus, son of Mary: this is a statement of the truth concerning which they doubt.

It befitteth not the Majesty of God that He should take unto Himself a son. Glory be to Him! When He decreeth a thing, He saith unto it only: Be! and it is.

And lo! God is my Lord and your Lord. So serve Him. That is the right path.

XIX: 16–36

AND MAKE mention in the Scripture of Moses. Lo! he was chosen, and he was a messenger of God, a prophet. We called him from the right slope of the Mount, and brought him nigh in communion.

And We bestowed upon him of Our mercy his brother Aaron, a prophet likewise.

XIX: 51–3

AND ARGUE not with the People of the Scripture unless it be in the most polite way, save with such of them as do wrong; and say: We believe in that which hath been revealed unto us and revealed unto you; our God and your God is One, and unto Him we surrender.

XXIX: 46

UNTO THIS, then, summon O Muhammad. And be thou upright as thou art commanded, and follow not their lusts, but say: I believe in whatever scripture God hath sent down, and I am commanded to be just among you. God is our Lord and your Lord. Unto us our works and unto you your works; no argument between us and you. God will bring us together, and unto Him is the journeying.

XLII: 15

THEN WE caused Our messengers to follow in their footsteps; and We caused Jesus, son of Mary, to follow, and gave him the Gospel, and placed compassion and mercy in the hearts of those who followed him. But monasticism they invented – We ordained it not for them – only seeking God's pleasure, and they observed it not with right observance.

LVII: 27

O PEOPLE OF the Scripture! Now hath Our messenger come unto you to make things plain unto you after a long interval between messengers, lest ye should say: There came not unto us a bearer of good tidings nor any warner. Now hath a messenger of cheer and a warner come unto you. God is Able to do all things.

V: 19

HUMANITY

RESPONSE TO REVELATION

OTHING OF Our revelation, even a single verse, do We abrogate or cause be forgotten, but We bring in its place one better or the like thereof. Knowest thou not that God is Able to do all things?

Knowest thou not that it is God unto Whom belongeth the Sovereignty of the heavens and the earth; and ye have not, beside God, any guardian or helper?

Or would ye question your messenger as Moses was questioned aforetime? He who chooseth disbelief instead of faith, verily he hath gone astray from a plain road.

II: 106–8

AY, O MUHAMMAD, to mankind: If ye love God, follow me; God will love you and forgive you your sins. God is Forgiving, Merciful.

Say: Obey God and the messenger. But if they turn away, lo! God loveth not the disbelievers in His guidance.

III: 31–2

AND VERILY We gave unto Moses the Scripture and We caused a train of messengers to follow after him, and We gave unto Jesus, son of Mary, clear proofs of God's sovereignty, and We supported him with the Holy spirit.

Is it ever so, that, when there cometh unto you a messenger from God with that which ye yourselves desire not, ye grow arrogant, and some ye disbelieve and some ye slay?

II: 87

AND WHEN Our clear revelations are recited unto them, they who look not for the meeting with Us say: Bring a Lecture other than this, or change it. Say O Muhammad: It is not for me to change it of my accord. I only follow that which is inspired in me. Lo! if I disobey my Lord I fear the retribution of an awful Day.

Say: If God had so willed I should not have recited it to you nor would He have made it known to you. I dwelt among you a whole lifetime before it came to me. Have ye then no sense?

X: 15–16

AND THEY say: If only he would bring us a miracle from his Lord! Hath there not come unto them the proof of what is in the former scriptures?

XX: 133

FOR INDEED it is not the eyes that grow blind, but it is the hearts, which are within the bosoms, that grow blind.
And they will bid thee hasten on the Doom, and God faileth not His promise, but lo! a Day with God is as a thousand years of what ye reckon.

XXII: 46–7

AND THE messenger saith: O my Lord! Lo! mine own folk make this Qur'an of no account.
Even so have We appointed unto every prophet an opponent from among the guilty; but God sufficeth for a Guide and Helper.

XXV: 30–1

THOSE WHO disbelieve say: This is naught but a lie that he hath invented, and other folk have helped him with it, so that they have produced a slander and a lie.

And they say: Fables of the men of old which he hath had written down so that they are dictated to him morn and evening.

Say unto them, O Muhammad: He who knoweth the secret of the heavens and the earth hath revealed it. Lo! He ever is Forgiving, Merciful.

And they say: What aileth this messenger of God that he eateth food and walketh in the markets? Why is not an angel sent down unto him, to be a warner with him.

Or why is not treasure thrown down unto him, or why hath he not a paradise from whence to eat? And the evil-doers say: Ye are but following a man bewitched.

See how they coin similitudes for thee, so that they are all astray and cannot find a road!

XXV: 4–9

YET THOSE who disbelieve say: When we have become dust like our fathers, shall we really be brought forth again?

We were promised this, before, we and our fathers. All this is naught but the fairy-tales of the ancients.

Say unto them, O Muhammad: Travel in the land and see how was the end of the sinners.

And grieve thou not for them, nor be in distress because of what they plot against thee.

And they say: When will this promise be fulfilled, if ye are truthful?

Say: It may be that a part of that which ye would hasten on is close behind you.

XXVII: 67–72

AND WE sent not unto any township a warner, but its pampered ones declared: Lo! we are disbelievers in that wherewith ye have been sent.

XXXIV: 34

THE BLIND man is not equal with the seer;
Nor is darkness tantamount to light;
Nor is the shadow equal with the sun's full
    heat;
Nor are the living equal with the dead. Lo!
    God maketh whom He will to hear.
    Thou canst not reach those who are in
    the graves.
Thou art but a warner.
Lo! We have sent thee with the Truth, a
    bearer of glad tidings and a warner; and
    there is not a nation but a warner hath
    passed among them.

And if they deny thee, those before them
    also denied.
Their messengers came unto them with
    clear proofs of God's Sovereignty, and
    with the Psalms and the Scripture
    giving light.
Then seized I those who disbelieved, and
    how intense was My abhorrence!

XXXV: 19–26

AND IF they deny thee, O Muhammad, messengers of God were denied before thee. Unto God all things are brought back.

XXXV: 4

AND THEY swore by God, their most binding oath, that if a warner came unto them they would be better guided than any of the earlier communities; yet, when a warner came unto them it aroused in them naught save repugnance.

XXXV: 42

AND THEY marvel that a warner from among themselves hath come unto them, and the disbelievers say: This is a wizard, a charlatan.

We have not heard of this in last religion. This is naught but an invention.

XXXVIII: 4,7

HAVE THEY not travelled in the land to see the nature of the consequence for those who disbelieved before them? They were mightier than these in power and in the traces which they left behind them in the earth. Yet God seized them for their sins, and they had no protector from God.

That was because their messengers kept bringing them clear proofs of God's Sovereignty but they disbelieved; so God seized them. Lo! He is Strong, severe in punishment.

XL: 21–2

AND VERILY Joseph brought you of old clear proofs, yet ye ceased not to be in doubt concerning what he brought you till, when he died, ye said: God will not send any messenger after him. Thus God deceiveth him who is a prodigal, a doubter.

XL: 34

HOW MANY a prophet did We send among
    the men of old!
And.never came there unto them a
    prophet but they used to mock him.

XLIII: 6–7

Response to Revelation ❧ 91

AND VERILY We had empowered them with that wherewith We have not empowered you, and had assigned them ears and eyes and hearts; but their ears and eyes and hearts availed them naught since they denied the revelations of God; and what they used to mock befell them.

XLVI: 26

EVEN SO there came no messenger unto those before them but they said: A wizard or a madman!
Have they handed down the saying as an heirloom one unto another? Nay, but they are an insolent people.
So withdraw from them O Muhammad, for thou art in no wise blameworthy, and warn, for warning profiteth believers.

LI: 52–5

AND WHEN Jesus son of Mary said: O Children of Israel! Lo! I am the messenger of God unto you, confirming that which was revealed before me in the Torah, and bringing good tidings of a messenger who cometh after me, whose name is the Praised One. Yet when he hath come unto them with clear proofs, they say: This is mere magic.

And who doeth greater wrong than he who inventeth a lie against God when he is summoned unto al-Islam? And God guideth not wrongdoing folk.

LXI: 6–7

FAIN WOULD they put out the light of God with their mouths, but God will perfect His light however much the disbelievers are averse.

He it is Who hath sent His messenger with the guidance and the religion of truth, that He may make it conqueror of all religion however much idolaters may be averse.

LXI: 8–9

ATTACHMENT TO THE WORLD

SAY: IF your fathers, and your sons, and your brethren, and your wives, and your tribe, and the wealth ye have acquired, and merchandise for which ye fear that there will be no sale, and dwellings ye desire are dearer to you than God and His messenger and striving in His way: then wait till God bringeth His command to pass. God guideth not wrongdoing folk.

IX: 24

O YE who believe! What aileth you that when it is said unto you: Go forth in the way of God, ye are bowed down to the ground with heaviness. Take ye pleasure in the life of the world rather than in the Hereafter? The comfort of the life of the world is but little in the Hereafter.

IX: 38

THIS LIFE of the world is but a pastime and a game. Lo! the home of the Hereafter – that is Life, if they but knew.

XXIX: 64

IT IS a promise of God. God faileth not His promise, but most of mankind know not.

They know only some appearance of the life of the world, and are heedless of the Hereafter.

Have they not pondered upon themselves? God created not the heavens and the earth, and that which is between them, save with truth and for a destined end. But truly many of mankind are disbelievers in the meeting with their Lord.

Have they not travelled in the land and seen the nature of the consequence for those who were before them? They were stronger than these in power, and they dug the earth and built upon it more than these have built. Messengers of their own came unto them with clear proofs of God's Sovereignty. Surely God wronged them not, but they did wrong themselves.

XXX: 6–9

SAY: SHALL We inform you who will be the greatest losers by their works? Those whose effort goeth astray in the life of the world, and yet they reckon that they do good work.

Those are they who disbelieve in the revelations of their Lord and in the meeting with Him. Therefore their works are vain, and on the Day of Resurrection We assign no weight to them.

XVIII: 103–5

AND WERE it not that mankind would have become one community, We might well have appointed, for those who disbelieve in the Beneficent, roofs of silver for their houses and stairs of silver whereby to mount,

And for their houses doors of silver and couches of silver whereon to recline, and ornaments of gold. Yet all that would have been but a provision of the life of the world. And the Hereafter with your Lord would have been for those who keep from evil.

XLIII: 33–5

KNOW THAT the life of the world is only play, and idle talk, and pageantry, and boasting among you, and rivalry in respect of wealth and children; as the likeness of vegetation after rain, whereof the growth is pleasing to the husbandman, but afterward it drieth up and thou seest it turning yellow, then it becometh straw. And in the Hereafter there is grievous punishment, and also forgiveness from God and His good pleasure, whereas the life of the world is but matter of illusion.

LVII: 20

RIVALRY IN worldly increase distracteth you
Until ye come to the graves.
Nay, but ye will come to know!
Again, nay, but ye will come to know!
Nay, would that ye knew now with a sure
    knowledge!
For ye will behold hell-fire.
Aye, ye will behold it with sure vision.
Then, on that day, ye will be asked
    concerning pleasure.

CII: 1–8

Attachment to the World ❧ 99

HE IS successful who cleansed himself,
And mentions the name of his Lord, and
prays,
But ye prefer the life of the world
Although the Hereafter is better and more
lasting.

LXXXVII: 14–17

WOE UNTO every slandering backbiter,
Who hath gathered wealth of this world
and arranged it.
He thinketh that his wealth will render him
immortal.
Nay, but verily he will be flung to the
Consuming One.
Ah, what will convey unto thee what the
Consuming One is!
It is the fire of God, kindled,
Which leapeth up over the hearts of men.
Lo! it is closed in on them
In outstretched columns.

CIV: 1–9

THE HUMAN SOUL

O YE WHO believe! Ye have charge of your own souls. He who erreth cannot injure you if ye are rightly guided. Unto God ye will all return; and then He will inform you of what ye used to do.

V: 105

E ACH SOUL earneth only on its own account, nor doth any laden bear another's load. Then unto your Lord is your return and He will tell you that wherein ye differed.

He it is Who hath placed you as viceroys of the earth and hath exalted some of you in rank above others, that He may try you by that which He hath given you. Lo! Thy Lord is swift in prosecution, and Lo! He verily is Forgiving, Merciful.

VI: 164–5

O YE who believe! Follow not the footsteps of the devil. Unto whomsoever followeth the footsteps of the devil, lo! he commandeth filthiness and wrong. Had it not been for the grace of God and His mercy unto you, not one of you would ever have grown pure. But God causeth whom He will to grow. And God is Hearer, Knower.

XXIV: 21

WE VERILY created man and We know what
    his soul
whisphereth to him, and We are nearer to him
    than his jugular vein.

L: 16

O YE WHO believe! Observe your duty to God. And let every soul look to that which it sendeth on before for the morrow. And observe your duty to God. Lo! God is Informed of what ye do.

And be not ye as those who forgot God, therefore He caused them to forget their souls. Such are the evil-doers.

LIX: 18–19

O MAN, VERILY you are ever toiling on toward your lord – painfully toiling – but you shall meet Him ... You shall surely travel from stage to stage.

LXXXIV: 6,19

AND A soul and Him Who perfected it
And inspired it with conscience of what is
    wrong and right.
He is indeed successful who purifies his
    soul,
And he is indeed a failure who corrupts it.

XCI: 7–10

THE LIFE BEYOND

LO! THOSE who purchase a small gain at the cost of God's covenant and their oaths, they have no portion in the Hereafter. God will neither speak to them nor look upon them on the Day of Resurrection, nor will He make them grow. Theirs will be a painful doom.

III: 77

NO SOUL can ever die except by God's leave and at a term appointed. Whoso desireth the reward of the world, We bestow on him thereof; and whoso desireth the reward of the Hereafter, We bestow on him thereof. We shall reward the thankful.

III: 145

IS ONE who followeth the pleasure of God as one who hath earned condemnation from God, whose habitation is the Fire, a hapless journey's end?

III: 162

AND THEY say: There is naught save our life of the world, and we shall not be raised again.
If thou couldst see when they are set before their Lord! He will say: Is not this real? They will say: Yea, verily, by our Lord! He will say: Taste now the retribution for that ye used to disbelieve.

They indeed are losers who deny their meeting with God until, when the Hour cometh on them suddenly, they cry: Alas for us, that we neglected it! They bear upon their backs their burdens. Ah, evil is that which they bear!

Naught is the life of the world save a pastime and a sport. Better far is the abode of the Hereafter for those who keep their duty to God. Have ye then no sense?

VI: 29–32

LO! THEY who deny Our revelations and scorn them, for them the gates of heaven will not be opened nor will they enter the Garden until the camel goeth through the needle's eye. Thus do We recompense the sinners.

Theirs will be a bed of hell, and over them coverings of hell. Thus do We recompense wrong-doers.

But as for those who believe and do good works – We tax not any soul beyond its capacity – such are rightful owners of the Garden. They abide therein.

And We remove whatever rancour may be in their hearts. Rivers flow beneath them. And they say: Praise belongs to God, Who hath guided us to this. We could not truly have been led aright if God had not guided us. Verily the messengers of our Lord did bring the Truth. And it is cried unto them: This is the Garden. Ye inherit it for what ye used to do.

And the dwellers of the Garden cry unto the dwellers of the Fire: We have found that which our Lord promised us to be the Truth. Have ye also found that which your Lord promised to be the Truth? They say: Yea, verily. And then a herald shall proclaim in between them: The curse of God is on evil-doers, who debar men from the path of God and would make it crooked, and who are disbelievers in the world to come.

VII: 40–5

GOD PROMISETH to the believers, men and women, Gardens underneath which rivers flow, wherein they will abide – blessed dwellings in Gardens of Eden. And far greater, God's good pleasure. That is the supreme triumph.

IX: 72

WE APPOINTED immortality for no mortal before thee. What! if thou diest, can they be immortal! Every soul must taste of death, and We try you with evil and with good, for ordeal. And unto Us ye will be returned.

XXI: 34–5

AND THOSE who disbelieve will not cease to be in doubt thereof until the Hour come upon them unawares, or there come unto them the doom of a disastrous day.
The Sovereignty on that day will be God's, He will judge between them. Then those who believed and did good works will be in Gardens of Delight.

XXII: 55–6

AND REMIND them of the Day when the Trumpet will be blown, and all who are in the heavens and the earth will start in fear, save him whom God willeth. And all come unto Him, humbled.

And thou seest the hills thou deemest solid flying with the flight of clouds: the doing of God Who perfecteth all things. Lo! He is Informed of what ye do.

Whoso bringeth a good deed will have better than its worth; and such are safe from fear that Day.

And whoso bringeth an ill-deed, such will be flung down on their faces in the Fire. Are ye rewarded aught save what ye did?

XXVII: 87–90

MEN ASK thee of the Hour. Say: The knowledge of it is with God only. What can convey the knowledge unto thee? It may be that the Hour is nigh.

Lo! God hath cursed the disbelievers, and hath prepared for them a flaming fire, wherein they will abide for ever. They will find then no protecting friend nor helper.

XXXIII: 63–5

AND MAKE mention of the day when the enemies of God are gathered unto the Fire, they are driven on till, when they reach it, their ears and their eyes and their skins testify against them as to what they used to do.

And they say unto their skins: Why testify ye against us? They say: God hath given us speech Who giveth speech to all things, and Who created you at the first, and unto Whom ye are returned.

Ye did not hide yourselves lest your ears and your eyes and your skins should testify against you, but ye deemed that God knew not much of what ye did.

That, your thought which ye did think about your Lord, hath ruined you; and ye find yourselves this day among the lost.

And though they are resigned, yet the Fire is still their home; and if they ask for favour, yet they are not of those unto whom favour can be shown.

XLI: 19–24

ND UNTO the evil-doer it is said: Thou wast in heedlessness of this. Now We have removed from thee thy covering, and piercing is thy sight this day.

L: 22

HE ASKETH: When will be this Day of
    Resurrection?
But when sight is confounded
And the moon is eclipsed
And sun and moon are united,
On that day man will cry: Whither to flee!
Alas! No refuge!
Unto thy Lord is the recourse that day.
On that day man is told the tale of that
    which he hath sent before and left
    behind.
Oh, but man is a telling witness against
    himself,
Although he tender his excuses.

LXXV: 6–15

SO WHEN the stars are put out,
And when the sky is riven asunder,
And when the mountains are blown away,
And when the messengers are brought
    unto their time appointed –
For what day is the time appointed?
For the Day of Decision.
And what will convey unto thee what the
    Day of Decision is! –
Woe unto the repudiators on that day!

LXXVII: 8–15

AND THE trumpet is blown, and all who are in the heavens and all who are in the earth swoon away, save him whom God willeth. Then it is blown a second time, and behold them standing waiting!

And the earth shineth with the light of her Lord, and the Book is set up, and the prophets and the witnesses are brought, and it is judged between them with truth, and they are not wronged.

XXXIX: 68–9

BUT WHEN the Great Catastrophe cometh,
The day when man will call to mind his
whole endeavour,
And hell will stand forth visible to him who
seeth,
Then, as for him who rebelled
And chose the life of the world,
Lo! hell will be his home.
But as for him who feared to stand before
his Lord and restrained his soul from
lust,
Lo! the Garden will be his home.
They ask thee of the Hour: when will it
come to port?
Why ask they? What hast thou to tell
thereof?
Unto thy Lord belongeth knowledge of the
term thereof.
Thou art but a warner unto him who
feareth it.
On the day when they behold it, it will be
as if they had but tarried for an evening
or the morn thereof.

LXXIX: 34–46

WHEN THE sun is overthrown,
And when the stars fall,
And when the hills are moved,
And when the camels big with young are
    abandoned,
And when the wild beasts are herded
    together,
And when the seas rise,
And when souls are reunited,
And when the girl-child that was buried
    alive is asked
For what sin she was slain,
And when the pages are laid open,
And when the sky is torn away,
And when hell is lighted,
And when the Garden is brought nigh,
Then every soul will know what it hath
    made ready.

LXXXI: 1–14

IN THAT day other faces will be calm,
Glad for their effort past,
In a high Garden
Where they hear no idle speech,
Wherein is a gushing spring,
Wherein are couches raised
And goblets set at hand
And cushions ranged
And silken carpets spread.

LXXXVIII: 8–16

THEN, AS for him whose scales are heavy
    with good works,
He will live a pleasant life.
But as for him whose scales are light,
A bereft and Hungry One will be his
    mother,
Ah, what will convey unto thee what
    she is! –
Raging Fire.

CI: 6–11

WHEN EARTH is shaken with her final
   earthquake
And Earth yieldeth up her burdens,
And man saith: What aileth her?
That day she will relate her chronicles,
Because thy Lord inspireth her.
That day mankind will issue forth in
   scattered groups to be shown their
   deeds.
And whoso doeth good an atom's weight
   will see it then,
And whoso doeth ill an atom's weight will
   see it then.

XCIX: 1–8

BUT WHEN the Blast shall sound
On the day when a man fleeth from his
    brother
And his mother and his father
And his wife and his children,
Every man that day will have concern
    enough to make him heedless of others.
On that day faces will be bright as dawn,
Laughing, rejoicing at good news;
And other faces, on that day, with dust
    upon them,
Veiled in darkness,
Those are the disbelievers, the wicked.

LXXX: 33–42

ISLAM IN DAILY LIFE

TRUE BELIEVER

THE FAITHFUL servants of the Beneficent are
    they who walk upon the earth modestly,
    and when the foolish ones address them
    answer: Peace;
And those who spend the night before
    their Lord, prostrate and standing,
And who say: Our Lord! Turn Thou from
    us the doom of hell;
Lo! the doom thereof is torment most
    terrible;
Lo! it is wretched as abode and station;
And those who, when they spend, are
    neither prodigal nor grudging;
and there is ever a just stand between the
    two;

And those who cry not unto any other god
    along with God,
nor take the life which God hath
    forbidden save in course of justice,
nor commit adultery – and whoso doeth
    this shall pay the penalty;

The doom will be doubled for him on the
Day of Resurrection,
and he will abide therein disdained for
ever;

Save him who repenteth and believeth
and doth righteous work;
as for such, God will change their evil
deeds to good deeds.
God is ever Forgiving, Merciful.
And whosoever repenteth and doeth good,
he verily repenteth toward God with true
repentance.
And those who will not bear false witness,
but when they pass by idle talk, pass by
with dignity.

And those who, when they are reminded
of the revelations of their Lord, fall not
deaf and blind thereat.
And who say: Our Lord! Vouchsafe us
comfort of our wives and of our
offspring, and make us a model to the
God-fearing.

They will be awarded with the highest
heaven, for that they endured
patiently, and they will be received
therein with welcome and peace.
Abiding there for ever. Happy is it as
abode and station!

XXV: 63–76

THE TRUE believers are those only who believe in God and His messenger and afterward doubt not, but strive with their wealth and their lives for the cause of God. Such are the sincere.

XLIX: 15

LO! MEN who surrender unto God, and
women who surrender,
and men who believe and women who
believe,
and men who obey and women who obey,
and men who speak the truth and women
who speak the truth,
and men who persevere in righteousness
and women who persevere,
and men who are humble and women who
are humble,
and men who give alms and women who
give alms,
and men who fast and women who fast,
and men who guard their modesty and
women who guard their modesty,
and men who remember God much and
women who remember –
God hath prepared for them forgiveness
and a vast reward.

XXXIII: 35

PRAYER AND DEVOTION

O MANKIND! CALL upon your Lord humbly and in secret. Lo! He loveth not aggressors.

Work not confusion in the earth after the fair ordering thereof and call on Him in fear and hope. Lo! the mercy of God is nigh unto the good.

VII: 55–6

THOSE WHO have believed and whose hearts have rest in the remembrance of God. Verily in the remembrance of God do hearts find rest!

Those who believe and do right: joy is for them, and bliss their journey's end.

XIII: 28–9

AND SAY not regarding anything: Lo! I shall
do that tomorrow,
But only, If God will.
And remember thy Lord when thou
forgettest, and say:
It may be that my Lord will guide me unto
a nearer way of truth than this.

XVIII: 23–4

RESTRAIN THYSELF along with those who cry unto their Lord at morn and evening, seeking His Countenance; and let not thine eyes overlook them, desiring the pomp of the life of the world; and obey not him whose heart We have made heedless of Our remembrance, who followeth his own lust and whose case hath been abandoned.

Say: It is the truth from the Lord of you all. Then whosoever will, let him believe, and whosoever will, let him disbelieve.

XVIII: 28–9

B UT HYMN the praise of thy Lord, and be of those who make prostration unto Him ...
And serve thy Lord till the Inevitable cometh unto thee.

XV: 98–9

T HEREFORE O Muhammad, be patient with what they say, and celebrate the praise of thy Lord ere the rising of the sun and ere the going down thereof. And glorify Him some hours of the night and at the two ends of the day, that thou mayst find
acceptance.

And strain not thine eyes to that We have given pairs of them to enjoy, the flower of the life of the world, that We may try them therein. The provision of thy Lord is better and more lasting.

And enjoin upon thy people worship, and be constant therein. We ask not of thee a provision, but it is We who provided for thee.

XX: 130–2

RECITE THAT which hath been inspired in thee of the Scripture, and establish worship. Lo! worship preserveth from lewdness and iniquity, but verily remembrance of God is more important. And God knoweth what ye do.

XXIX: 45

AND WHEN they mount upon the ships they pray to God, making their faith pure for Him only, but when He bringeth them safe to land, behold! they ascribe partners unto Him, that they may disbelieve in that which We have given them, and that they may take their ease. But they will come to know.

XXIX: 65–6

AND VERILY We gave Luqman wisdom, saying: Give thanks unto God; and whosoever giveth thanks, he giveth thanks for the good of his soul. And whosoever refuseth – lo! God is Absolute, Owner of Praise.

XXXI: 12

OYE WHO believe!
Remember God with much remembrance.
And glorify Him early and late.
He it is Who blesseth you, and His angels bless you, that He may bring you forth from darkness unto light; and He is ever Merciful to the believers.

Their salutation on the day when they shall meet Him will be: Peace. And He hath prepared for them a goodly recompense.

XXXIII: 41–4

SO WAIT patiently O Muhammad for thy Lord's decree, for surely thou art in Our sight; and hymn the praise of thy Lord when thou uprisest, and in the night-time also hymn His praise, and at the setting of the stars.

LII: 48–9

PERSONAL CONDUCT

Good Deeds

AS FOR that Abode of the Hereafter
We assign it unto those who seek not
 oppression in the earth, nor yet
 corruption.
The sequel is for those who ward off evil.
Whoso bringeth a good deed, he will have
 better than the same;
while as for him who bringeth an ill-deed,
 those who do ill-deeds
will be recompensed only for what they
 did.

XXVIII: 83–4

IT IS NOT righteousness that ye turn your
   faces to the East and the West;
but righteous is he who believeth in God
   and the Last Day
and the angels and the Scripture and the
   prophets;
and giveth wealth, for love of Him, to
   kinsfolk
and to orphans and the needy and the
   wayfarer
and to those who ask, and to set slaves free;
and observeth proper worship and payeth
   the poor-due.
And those who keep their treaty when they
   make one,
and the patient in tribulation and
   adversity and time of stress.
Such are they who are sincere. Such are
   the God-fearing.

II: 177

WHOSO BRINGETH a good deed will receive tenfold the like thereof, while whoso bringeth an ill-deed will be awarded but the like thereof; and they will not be wronged.

VI: 160

FULFIL THE covenant of God when ye have
covenanted,
and break not your oaths after confirming
them,
and after ye have made God surety over
you.
Lo! God knoweth what ye do.

XVI: 91

SAY: I am only a mortal like you. My Lord inspireth in me that your God is only One God. And whoever hopeth for the meeting with his Lord, let him do righteous work, and make none sharer of the worship due unto his Lord.

XVIII: 110

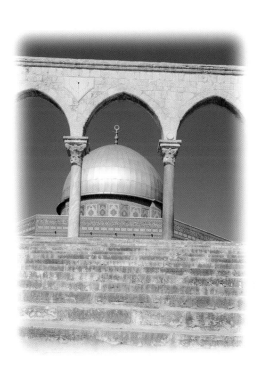

WEALTH AND children are an ornament of the life of the world. But the good deeds which endure are better in thy Lord's sight for reward, and better in respect of hope.

XVIII: 46

O YE WHO believe! Let not one group of men among you deride another, for they may be better than them, nor one group of women deride another who may be better than them; neither defame one another, nor insult one another by nicknames. How bad it is to call each other by bad names after all of you became believers. And whoso turneth not in repentance from this, such are the unjust ones.

O ye who believe! Shun much suspicion; for lo! some suspicion is a crime. And spy not, neither backbite one another. Would one of you love to eat the flesh of his dead brother? Ye abhor that so abhor the other! And keep your duty to God. God is Relenting, Merciful.

O mankind! We have created you male and female, and have made you nations and tribes that ye may know one another. Lo! the noblest of you, in the sight of God, is the best in conduct. God is All-Knower, All-Aware.

XLIX: 11–13

AND WHOSOEVER striveth, striveth only for himself,

for lo! God is altogether Independent of His creatures.

And as for those who believe and do good works,

We shall remit from them their evil deeds and shall repay them the best that they did.

XXIX: 6–7

O YE WHO believe! Why say ye that which ye do not? It is most hateful in the sight of God that ye say that which ye do not.

LXI: 2–3

L O! MAN is a state of loss, save those who believe and do good works, and exhort one another to truth and exhort one another to endurance.

CIII: 2–3

Helping Others

O YE WHO believe! spend of that wherewith We have provided you ere a day come when there will be no trafficking, nor friendship, nor intercession. The disbelievers, they are the wrong-doers.

II: 254

T HE LIKENESS of those who spend their wealth in God's way is as the likeness of a grain which groweth seven ears, in every ear a hundred grains. God giveth increase manifold to whom He will. God is All-Embracing, All-Knowing.

II: 261

T HE WEALTH you invest in usury so that it should grow at the expense of other people's wealth, does not grow in the sight of God, but that which you give in charity, seeking God's Countenance, it is multiplied several-fold.

XXX: 39

A KIND WORD with forgiveness is better than almsgiving followed by injury. God is Absolute, Clement.

O ye who believe! Render not vain your almsgiving by reproach and injury, like him who spendeth his wealth only to be seen of men and believeth not in God and the Last Day. His likeness is as the likeness of a rock whereon is dust of earth; a rainstorm smiteth it, leaving it smooth and bare. They have no control of aught of that which they have gained. God guideth not the disbelieving folk.

And the likeness of those who spend their wealth in search of God's pleasure, and for the strengthening of their souls, is as the likeness of a garden on a height. The rainstorm smiteth it and it bringeth forth its fruit twofold. And if the rainstorm smite it not, then the shower. God is Seer of what ye do.

Would any of you like to have a garden of palm-trees and vines, with rivers flowing underneath it, with all kinds of fruit for him therein; and old age hath stricken him and he hath feeble offspring; and a fiery whirlwind striketh it and it is all consumed by fire? Thus God maketh plain His revelations unto you, in order that ye may give thought.

II: 263–6

I F YE publish your almsgiving, it is well, but if ye hide it and give it to the poor, it will be better for you, and will atone for some of your ill-deeds. God is Informed of what ye do.

And whatsoever good thing ye spend, it is for yourselves, when ye spend not save in search of God's Countenance; and whatsoever good thing ye spend, it will be repaid to you in full, and ye will not be wronged.

II: 271–2

A ND LET not those who possess dignity and ease among you swear not to give to the near of kin and to the needy, and to fugitives for the cause of God.
Let them forgive and show indulgence.
Yearn ye not that God may forgive you?
God is Forgiving, Merciful.

XXIV: 22

A ND WHOSO is saved from his own selfishness – such are they who are successful.

LIX: 9

O YE WHO believe! Let not your wealth nor your children distract you from remembrance of God. Those who do so, they are the losers.

And spend of that wherewith We have provided you before death cometh unto one of you and he saith: My Lord! If only thou wouldst reprieve me for a little while, then I would give alms and be among the righteous.

But God reprieveth no soul when its term cometh, and God is Informed of what ye do.

LXIII: 9–11

HAST THOU observed him who belieth
    religion?
That is he who repelleth the orphan,
And urgeth not the feeding of the needy.
Ah, woe unto worshippers
Who are heedless of their prayer;
Who would be seen at worship
Yet refuse small kindnesses!

CVII: 1–7

Good Words

A GOODLY SAYING, is as a goodly tree, its root
set firm, its branches reaching into
heaven,
Giving its fruit at every season by
permission of its Lord.
God coineth the similitudes for mankind
in order that they may reflect.
And the similitude of a bad saying is as a
bad tree,
uprooted from upon the earth, possessing
no stability.

XIV: 24–6

BUT WHEN ye enter houses, salute one another with a
greeting from God, blessed and sweet. Thus God maketh
clear His revelations for you, that haply ye may
understand.

XXIV: 61

Respect for Parents

SET NOT up with God any other god lest thou sit down condemned and forsaken.

Thy Lord hath decreed, that ye worship none save Him, and that ye show kindness to parents. If one of them or both of them attain old age with thee,

say not Fie unto them nor repulse them, but speak unto them a gracious word.

And lower unto them the wing of humbleness through mercy, and say: My Lord! Have mercy on them both as they did care for me when I was little.

XVII: 22–4

Patience

O YOU WHO believe, seek courage in patience and prayer, for God is with those who are patient and persevere.

II: 153

Humility

AND WALK not boisterously upon the earth.
Verily thou will not make a hole in the
   earth,
nor attain the mountains in height.

XVII: 37

AND REMEMBER when Luqman said unto his son, when he was exhorting him ... O my dear son! Perform the prayer and enjoin kindness and forbid iniquity, and bear patiently whatever may befall thee. Lo! that is true constancy.

Turn not thy cheek away from men in scorn, nor walk in the land exultantly. God loveth not any man proud and boastful.

XXXI: 13,17–18

Justice

O YE WHO believe! It is not lawful for you forcibly to inherit the women of your deceased kinsmen, nor that ye should put constraint upon them that ye may take away a part of that which ye have given them, unless they be guilty of flagrant lewdness. But consort with them in kindness, for if ye hate them it may happen that ye hate a thing wherein God hath placed much good.

And if ye wish to exchange one wife for another and ye have given unto one of them a sum of money (however great), take nothing from it. Would ye take it by the way of calumny and open wrong?

How can ye take it back when you have fondly met each other in intimacy, and they have taken a strong pledge from you?

IV: 19–21

O YE WHO believe! Be ye staunch in justice, witnesses for God, even though it be against yourselves or your parents or your kindred, whether the case be of a rich man or a poor man, for God is near unto both of them. So follow not passion lest ye lapse from truth and if ye lapse or fall away, then lo! God is ever Informed of what ye do.

IV: 135

TESTS AND DIFFICULTIES

G OD TASKETH not a soul beyond its scope. For it is only that which it hath earned, and against it only that which it hath deserved. Our Lord! Condemn us not if we forget, or miss the mark!

Our Lord! Lay not on us such a burden as thou didst lay on those before us! Our Lord! Impose not on us that which we have not the strength to bear! Pardon us, absolve us and have mercy on us, Thou, our Protector, and give us victory over the disbelieving folk.

II: 286

WHATEVER OF good befalleth thee. O man, it is from God, and whatever of ill befalleth thee it is from thyself.

IV: 79

L O! GOD wrongs not men in anything; but men wrong themselves.

X: 44

G OD SAID: O Iblis! What aileth thee that thou art not among the prostrate?
He said: I am not one to prostrate myself unto a mortal whom Thou hast created out of potter's clay of black mud altered!

He said: Then go thou forth from hence, for lo! thou art outcast.

And lo! the curse shall be upon thee till the Day of Judgement.

He said: My Lord! Reprieve me till the day when they are raised.

He said: Then lo! thou art of those reprieved till the Day of appointed time.

He said: My Lord! Because Thou hast sent me astray, I verily shall adorn the path of error for them in the earth, and shall mislead them every one,

Save such of them as are Thy perfectly devoted servants.

XV: 32–40

AND IF we cause man to taste some mercy from Us and afterward withdraw it from him, lo! he is despairing, thankless.

And if We cause him to taste grace after some misfortune that had befallen him, he saith: The ills have gone from me. Lo! he is exultant, boastful; save those who persevere and do good works. Theirs will be forgiveness and a great reward.

XI: 9–11

DO MEN imagine that they will be left at ease because they say, We believe, and will not be tested with affliction?

Lo! We tested those who were before you. Thus God knoweth those who are sincere, and knoweth those who feign.

Or do those who do ill-deeds imagine that they can outstrip Us? Ill they judge.

Whoso looketh forward to the meeting with God let him know that God's reckoning is surely nigh, and He is the Hearer, the Knower.

XXIX: 2–5

MAN TIRETH not of praying for good, and if ill toucheth him, then he is disheartened, desperate.

And verily, if We cause him to taste mercy after some hurt that hath touched him, he will say: This is my own; and I deem not that the Hour will ever rise, and if I am brought back to my Lord, I surely shall be better off with Him – But We verily shall tell those who disbelieve all that they did, and We verily shall make them taste hard punishment.

When We show favour unto man, he withdraweth and turneth aside, but when ill toucheth him then he aboundeth in prayer.

XLI: 49–51

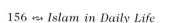

LO! MAN was created anxious,
Fretful when evil befalleth him
And, when good befalleth him, grudging;
Save worshippers.
Who are constant at their worship
And in whose wealth there is a right
  acknowledged
For the beggar and the destitute;
And those who believe in the Day of
  Judgement,
And those who are fearful of their Lord's
  doom –
Lo! the doom of their Lord is that before
  which none can feel secure –
And those who preserve their chastity.

LXX: 19–29

AS FOR man, whenever his Lord trieth him
    by honouring him, and is gracious unto
    him, he saith: My Lord honoureth me.
But whenever He trieth him by
    straitening his means of life, he saith:
    My Lord despiseth me
Nay, but ye for your part honour not the
    orphan
And urge not on the feeding of the poor.
And ye devour heritages with devouring
    greed.
And love wealth with abounding love.

                                    LXXXIX: 15–20